Meditations on My Mountain

Jon D. Newbill RScP

Mishal,
I cannot help you on
your path.
May you be inspired
to find your own "Shoes"
I'll see you at The
Top of the Mountain
Namaste,
Jon

i

First published in 2016

Copyright © 2016 by Jon D. Newbill RScP

ISBN 978-1-329-81039-6

Published by Jon D. Newbill RScP

You can contact Jon at jond@bitworkssystems.com

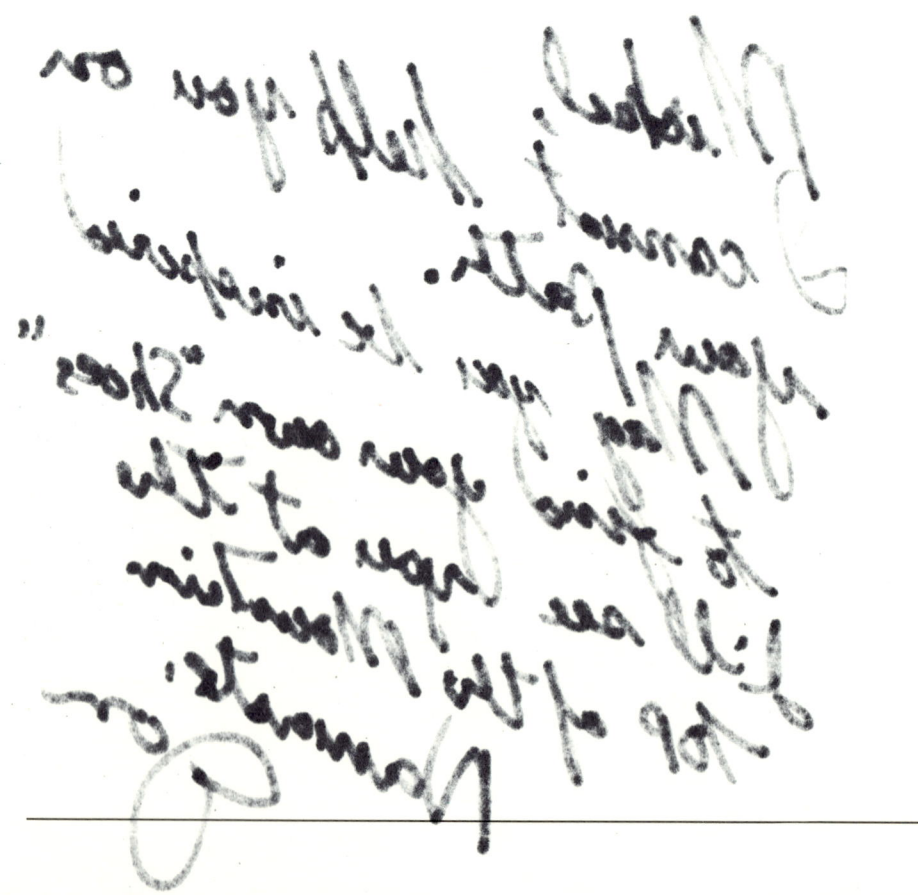

Contents

Contents

Contents

Contents

Contents

Contents

Foreword

January 4th, 2016

In southern California at the west end of Simi Valley, Mount McCoy (1325 feet) overlooks all of Simi Valley, Moorpark and Thousand Oaks. It has been a landmark since the early 1800's and has had a cross on top since that time. The current twelve foot white concrete cross was placed there in 1941.

I climbed Mount McCoy for the first time in January 2005, nearly 30 years after first moving to Simi Valley. It was the day I made my first entry in my journal of awakening. I had lived in Simi Valley without really knowing it. In the past eleven years I have climbed this mountain well over one hundred times. In that time we have become fast and trusted friends. We have become intimates who know each other well.

There is a very large bolder known as Easter Island Rock about half-way up on the steeper northern route. There are thirteen switchbacks on the easier southern route, nine on the adjacent hill and four after crossing to the hill itself. For several years there was a "heart rock" embedded in the trail at switchback eight and three quarters although I haven't seen it recently. Bowling ball sized rocks mark the end of switchbacks three and six. Switchback nine is the longest. Switchback twelve is shortest and has a shortcut to bypass it.

Yes, we know each other well. In eleven years much has changed in my life and the Mountain has remained. It has always been there for me to climb and I have climbed it in anger and joy, in sickness and in health, in despair and exhilaration. I have walked up it, hiked up it, run up it, picnicked on it, prayed on it and most of all meditated on it, and so it is, that I have come to affectionately call it my Mountain.

Six years ago I came to live at the base of My Mountain. At the time I didn't realize it was for me to become closer to My Mountain. This book is a compilation of poems, prayers and thoughts along the way up. Yet, my Mountain is not a destination. It's about the climb. The Mountain and I both know the climb begins anew each day. For there are no endings without new beginnings or as I like to say every day is a "BegEnding."

Top of Mount McCoy

January 22nd, 2005

I hiked the trail to the top of Mount McCoy for the first time this morning. I saw many of God's creatures. I saw moss on the rocks, sagebrush, anise, mountain mahogany, black sage, buckwheat and a yellow flower I don't know the name of. I'm now sitting on the bench at the top of the trail just below the cross. The Sun is up and reflecting on Sinaloa Lake. There is a small boat on the lake.

A flock of ducks or geese just flew by going northwest. I am sitting here looking over all of Simi Valley. There is a low haze which partially obscures the features of the valley making it all the more magnificent.

A Brighter Day

June 3rd, 2005

One year ago this day my mother left this Earth. I measure my spiritual growth from that day. I think my spiritual growth was limited until I no longer had parents to fall back on. Each day is like a grain of sand falling through the hour glass of life, three hundred sixty five in a year. How much progress can be made in a day? How much in a year? How much can we change? How much in just an instant? For progress begins in one instant, that instant we decide we are at choice. Our choice! In the Absolute of Being there is no such thing as time or space just an I am-ness and that is enough.

Progress is not linear. It's like evolution, stagnating for what seems like an eternity and then suddenly bang there's a flash and you're racing up the mountain, amazed at your own progress. Then a year has passed and you pause and look back and see how far you've come. How joyful it is to see the path you have made. How exhilarating to see others inspired to find their way up the mountain, some following your path, some making their own, but all on an upward journey. Looking up you see there is more mountain to climb, the journey is always upward. More Awareness more Peace and more Inner Truth still to be revealed.

I thank you for all you have given me. For the lessons you taught me even while I was asleep. I love you. Namaste.

I Love with Ease

July 5th, 2005

The Divine Force of the Universe is All Ways giving. All is natural and at One with the Universe. All of nature works in harmony without conflict. Each living creature in nature gives and receives in balance with the One.   All power and knowledge is available through the Divine Force. Like inhaling and exhaling each draws what it needs and returns Love to the Universe.

I too am one with the Divine and live in balance. My every action exhibits a calm Love of Being.   When discord may appear I recognize the One and know that Love is the highest vibration and that includes me! As I go through my day I see everyone and everything as being in harmony with the Universe in a perfect interchange and circulation of life. I know this as Truth right now and overflow with Joy for the Presence of the Divine throughout my Being.   I live my life with Love and Compassion, knowing that all I require is supplied with ease. There is no forcing or controlling for Source is Infinite and has no limitations whatsoever!

I release this with the Love I know is mine. And so it is

Of Space, Light and Spheres

November 12th, 2005

I first heard this thought of history, flowing out forever from everything from Dennis Nicholson, a piano tuner, 20 years ago. He has since left this earth plane. I remember thinking how crazy what he was saying sounded, which illustrates the following quote from *Sidartha* by Hermann Hesse.

"Wisdom is not communicable. The wisdom which a wise man tries to communicate always sounds foolish."

How can light travel though space? If there is nothing in space then what is it that is traveling? Sound travels as waves of compressed air. Air is the medium that propagates the waves. But light travels out in all directions with no apparent medium to propagate the waves. Is there, as Einstein thought in the 1920's but was unable to prove, a form of Ether even in the vacuum of space? To think that at some point in the Universe from some distant world with a telescope of unimaginable power one could observe the entire history of Earth starting right now.

At some point in space every moment in Earth's history exists right now. Like a river of light it flows; the Chi of the earth flowing back to its Source. All moments existing at the same time yet at each point always changing. The beginning of the earth pours out at the outermost reaches of the Universe

6

occupying a sphere of inconceivable size, billions of light years in diameter. Yet that beginning is connected through the vast space back to or should I say forward to this moment emanating from Earth's ever present now.

I view this Light Sphere as the Spirit of Earth continually expanding, moving, spiraling, upward and outward. Then I think of all the billions of other worlds in the Universe. All these worlds with their own expanding Sphere of Light. All of these Light Spheres are overlapping in the Universe and all continuing to expand and yet Space that holds them does not fill up. Even worlds that no longer exist have a Light Sphere that continues to expand. Is this immortality?

In the night sky I see many stars. I am experiencing one infinitesimal point on their expanding Light Sphere. I am here in my Now and all of these Light Spheres are flowing past me truly at the speed of light! Before Earth began its Light journey through Space many of these stars exploded and others still exist. From my vantage point both types are indistinguishable from each other. There is no difference in their Light as I perceive it. This makes me ask, "Is death the end"? Is not each of these worlds merely transitioning into a Light in order to expand out to Infinity? What a mystery this Universe is. How exciting to live in that mystery.

Christmas Treasure

December 30th, 2005

Sometimes on a treasure hunt you find a treasure other than the one you're looking for. I found this a while looking for our passports for our cruise in January. It was handwritten on a lined pad. The first few pages were in Spanish from when Mom was taking a Spanish class. I was about to throw it out but decided to check a few pages further.

Sung to the tune of Jingle Bells by Lena Mae Newbill
date unknown (sometime in late 1990's or early 2000's)

Can you, can you see
The love-light in my eyes
It's shining there because
I am an angel in disguise

God is the life in me
And every living thing
It's God who makes the flowers bloom
And all the birds to sing.

Yes I know, yes I know
God is All there is
Oh how it is great to know
God is all there is.

God is the Power in me

I use it every day
I use it when I dance and sing
And when I work or play

God is the love in me
And love is what I give
I give with All my
heart and soul
I give that I might live

In his love, In his love
In his love divine
Oh, how great it _is_ to live
In his love divine

At Christmas time
That time of year
My heart's so full of Love and Cheer
I'll wrap it up in ribbons blue
And give all with love to you.

Merry Christmas.

That's Odd

May 17th, 2006

My birthday has only odd numbers in it 3-1-1957

The time I was born has only odd numbers in it 3:47 PM

All three of my names have an odd number of letters.

Jon Douglas Newbill

How odd that I've lived nearly half a century and only just

become aware of this.

Beyond Sense

July 7th, 2006

When the air is fresh,

the nose receives the fragrance of Life.

When the air is clear,

the eye can see to infinity.

When the air is still,

the ear can hear the voice of God.

When the tongue ceases to be hungry,

it can taste the sweetness of Life.

When the heart no longer needs to feel love in return,

it knows Love for all humanity.

Attachment or Commitment

October 6th, 2006

The question is, "When pursuing a goal or desire, how can I know the difference between commitment and attachment?" That is, attachment to something that no longer serves me? Can one turn into the other?

Intuitively I desire to be committed to my goals but not with unhealthy attachment. Does this mean I'm attached to commitment? Or am I committed to not being too attached? Ah the paradox. Be still my Mind and listen. Listen . . .

In stillness I let go and let God and a quiet reverent voice says "Attachment is fear, Commitment is Love." Attachment is putting the focus on the possibility of loss. Commitment comes from truly loving the desire I am committed to create and if I perish in the process then I perish but what a Joy to have the committed experience with no fear of the possibility of failure. At times I may fail, but without attachment I no longer fear failure. Commitment means I know that from that failure there is a new strength and Infinite Power. Commitment knows that despite the outcome the Universe supports me.

"Yea though I walk through the valley of the shadow of death I will fear no evil" Psalms 23:4

Thank you God for teaching me even when I was attached.

The Math of Love

December 5th, 2006

Love is not addition; two halves do not make a whole. One person can never complete the other. Both must be complete to start with. Love multiplies but when you multiply two values that are less than a whole you get less than you started with. A half times a half is a quarter. This is what happens when two people expect the other to fulfill all their needs and desires. Eventually each finds they have less than they started with. On the other hand when both are complete at the beginning then together they are still whole. A whole multiplied by a whole is still fully whole 1 x 1 = 1. Realizing this is the secret to Peace on the planet. You cannot make your partner, your family, your friends or the planet whole, the answer is for each of us to discover the feeling of wholeness within our Self.

True Love is Blind

December 19th, 2006

"True love is blind", it's a cliché. I've heard it my whole life. I have heard it so much that I took it for granted. I accepted it as a truism. When you're first in love you don't see things as they "really are". You see through rose colored glasses, see things as you desire them to be, as perfect, without flaws. In time however when the honeymoon is over you see the reality of that which you love. I always saw that period of blindness as a negative, that the process of not seeing things as they "really are" was something to be avoided. The objective was to get to that second stage of seeing the "reality" of things as quickly as possible. To live in that blind state was a delusion.

This morning I began to wonder about this "truism" and came to a new awareness. My truth came in the realization that after many years of living with "reality" that I had merely exchanged the rose colored glasses for ones that were dirty and smudged. Truth is what we see and believe in our heart. There is no absolute reality "out there". Knowing that is like putting the rose colored glasses back on but doing it consciously. Truth, is knowing that it is my choice to wear them. It is my choice to see the world as beautiful, magnificent and wondrous. To see the world in that way is just as True as any other view I choose. In a sense it's like seeing more clearly through the rose tint. No longer ignoring those things which I saw as ugly reality with the smudged glasses but knowing there is a higher Truth and seeing all with loving rosiness.

The Gifted Mirror

January 19th, 2007

I received a gift today, a perfect flawless mirror. But, when I looked in it what I saw was far from perfect. What I saw frightened me and I turned away from it. I thought it ugly and wished for it to go away. To look caused me pain. So I ran and hide from my mirror gift.

I felt alone and so I came back. When I looked again I thought to make the image more pleasant. I took out my pen and drew a smile over the image. But every time I moved the smile didn't line up and the image beneath seemed more frightening hiding behind the false smile of a clown.

I made a drawing of myself smiling in a garden and covered over my mirror gift with it so I no longer could see the frightful image beneath. The picture was lovely and I enjoyed looking at it. It lifted my Spirit, … for a time. But after a while my thoughts returned to what was still beneath the image. I became curious if the ugly image was still there. I had to know. I peeled back the drawing and peeked below. And there it was. The same clown face more terrifying than before. The image in my perfect mirror gift had grown more hideous in my absence.

I became angry that my gift was causing me such pain. I shouted at my gift "How dare you" and attacked the ugly image with my fist. The glass broke and cut my hand. I cried out. As

I stared at the broken pieces on the floor the ugly image was still there, staring at me from a prison of glass shards. I picked up the largest shard and began to look at it. And as I looked I began to laugh. I laughed and laughed and laughed. And as I did the ugly image vanished. I saw the most beautiful smile I'd ever seen.

What a miracle a mirror is. It is a most beautiful gift. For in it I see my Self. It reflects, and in so doing allows me to reflect also. Reflect on who I am. If I don't like what I see and attack the image I hurt my Self. In life how often I've tried to put on the false smile, or cover up true feelings. And yet when I learn to laugh at myself the ugliness vanishes.

Thank you to all the reflectors in my life who allows me to see myself. They are my Gifted Mirror for teaching me to laugh.

Know That I Love You

July 3rd, 2007

When you tell me I'm wrong

Know that I Love you

When you tell me I'm right

Know that I Love you

When we quarrel

Know that I Love you

When we rejoice

Know that I Love you

When I make you sad

Know that I Love you

When I make you happy

Know that I Love you

When I don't meet your expectations

Know that I Love you

When I fulfill your heart desires

Know that I Love you

When I hurt you

Know that I Love you

When you hurt me

Know that I Love you

When I make you pissed

Know that I Love you

When I cause you bliss

Know that I Love you

When we are apart

Know that I Love you

When I am with you,

even when I forget to say it

Know that I Love you

When I make you mad

Know that I Love you

When I make you glad

Know that I Love you

When I cause you pain

Know that I Love you

When I cause you Joy

Know that I Love you

Know that I Love you

Not for what others think you are

Know that I Love you

Not for what you think you are

Know that I Love you

Not for what I think you are

Know That I Love you

For what I know you to BE

Know that I Love you

For the Light within you

The Light within you always

The Light you are with all your flaws

The Light you are, even at times when my shaded glasses fail to

see it

Know that I choose to Love you

Because when I see that Light it fills my heart up to overflowing

When I choose to Love you

My Life is filled with Light

Thank you for being in my Life

And lighting my Life

The Roller Coaster

August 11th, 2007

Assignment: Pick two of the most different things you can think of and write of them as one.

As usual I left writing for the Write Stuff Writers group until just before the meeting. I had thought some on the concept over the past month but not much. So as I do before I write, I began to meditate about an hour before the meeting. I let stillness come. I sat in silence listening to music. And then I sat in silence listening to my head. I began to chase my thoughts away. My intention was to empty out in order to be filled up. As I worked on emptying I found more thoughts appearing. Then I remembered not to resist. Not to push against the ideas. To empty I must let ideas fill my head. So in a moment I became a thought machine, a racing turning churning thought machine. Flowing with every thought that came to mind following each one to see where it would go. Letting it go, watching it go. I was having a wild ride on my thoughts. I thought of mountains and climbing them and rocks and falling and flying and birds and fish and whales and amoebas and life and oneness and separateness and Love and hate and how similar they are and my children and how different they are and my love and how human we all are when the light in each of us shines. I thought of this assignment and how easy it is to be different and how hard it is to be alike and how no two of us are

19

alike and how all of us are the same. I was riding a roller coaster of thoughts. The thrill of adventure, each moment another unexpected turn around the corner of the unknown. Not knowing where the next thought was going to take me and fearful where it might lead. Is this safe? Could I get hurt on this uncontrolled tsunami of thoughts? Could that next thought take me over the top and send me crashing down to the depths of despair? Am I out of control? Am I thinking thoughts or are thoughts thinking me? Am I just along for the ride? . . . . And then as suddenly as the ride had started it stopped. There was silence. There was total stillness. Then came the tears . . . tears of Joy. The assignment is done.

Love and Law

January 25th, 2008

Man's laws are made by and for

those who have not yet learned how to Love

Happiness

February 6th, 2008

The simplest way to be happy,

and yet perhaps the most difficult,

is to change what I want

Intuition

February 19th, 2008

Call it Instinct, Intuition or

that Small Still Voice,

When I am quiet and listen and follow it

my soul rejoices in my alignment with the Divine.

Nightmares

February 20th, 2008

Nightmares are soul messengers

pointing to areas of highest potential for my soul's growth;

Where facing my greatest fears shall yield

my greatest hidden treasures

Heart Light

February 20th, 2008

When my heart begins to glow

it's then I know

which way to go.

For when my heart is filled with Light

I conquer my fear without might.

Upward Spiral

February 25th, 2008

When you get to the top,

there's always more . . .

Seeing in the Dark

February 25th, 2008

Loving anything is just a matter of looking

long enough into the dark, in spite of my fear,

until I see the shining glimmer of the dawn.

Dreams

February 29th, 2008

Dreams are the after-burners of Life,

They power me to new heights

Above all clouds of doubt

Freedom and Happiness

March 6th, 2008

When I can believe in my truth and yours

though they appear to contradict,

yet not betray my own or feel compelled

to have you believe my truth,

then I am free . . . free to be happy

Wanting What's Important

March 11th, 2008

I've stopped putting artificial sweetener in my tea. This morning I notice the warmth of my tea. This morning I notice the spices in my tea. This morning I notice what I think I want isn't important at all. It only hides what really is important. This morning I prayed for the driver of the overturned car on the freeway

United

March 29th, 2008

Finding blame separates

Finding solutions Unites

I fly United

Laughter

April 1st, 2008

Laughter is the pick that cracks open the shell of the ego

Shoes

April 3rd, 2008

I cannot help you on your path,

though I would gladly give my shoes

to ease your journey.

Alas mine would not fit you

and the kind act though good intentioned

shall be misinterpreted.

You must find your own shoes.

The Master Cobbler makes each pair custom.

One must meet him face to face with confidence

and demand a pair to match

the feet you were given

and the path you have chosen.

Only then shall we meet

where our two separate paths join

at the top of the Mountain.

Creative Spark

April 4th, 2008

The creative spark of inspiration catches fire

in the deepest moments of meditation and tranquility

when the mind is quiet and receptive to the

Infinite Knowledge of the Universe.

Wisdom

April 5th, 2008

Wisdom does not come with age.

Wisdom comes with painful experience.

My pride, selfishness, arrogance, fear and anger

are all my teachers of Wisdom.

Commitment

April 7th, 2008

The difference between attachment and commitment is like

The difference between pushing water and letting it flow

Dark Secrets

April 11th, 2008

My darkest secrets are not secrets.

Secrets must be hidden from view,

But like Poe's telltale heart I unknowingly

Display my secrets to the world with my every action.

Opinions

April 18th, 2008

Fleeting though they are the most precious moments

occur when my mind is free from opinions

In these moments I feel more deeply,

hear more clearly and

see further than ever

into the Great Mystery of Life

Lifting Paradox

April 21st, 2008

To lift up others I must first

Climb out of my own pit of despair

Yet the best way out of my own pit

Is to lift up another

Hurry Down

April 24th, 2008

When I hurry-up I run

Run from Now to get to the future

I never get to the future

That brings me down

I can't hurry-up

I can only hurry-down

Anger

April 30th, 2008

I once thought my anger a powerful tool.

Alas, it is like making fine cabinetry with an ax.

Watch Carefully

May 9th, 2008

Watch carefully

There are no missteps in my Life

Watch carefully

Each misstep is necessary

Watch carefully

Each misstep is opportunity knocking

Watch carefully

At the next fork

Watch carefully

How I choose anew

Fear

May 14th, 2008

I cannot escape my fear by running from it.

It is like running from my shadow.

As I move into the light

on every step it is tethered behind me

like a helpful friend urging me on

to move further towards the Light.

No Recall

May 28th, 2008

If you ask me to recount
all acts that I have forgiven
I must answer I don't know
for if I can recall the act
I haven't forgiven

Creation

June 6th, 2008

Feel it in your Heart
See it in your Mind
Experience it in the world

Light

June 9th, 2008

If I can see at all
I am not in total darkness
and where there is some Light
more is always possible,
so I seek to open up the place
where the Light enters my Life.

Reality

June 12th, 2008

Ultimately all reality exists in my mind.

Once I fully embody this I am free.

Free to create a world of my wildest dreams.

Fully embodied in this concept no harm can touch me

or anyone I Love.

Success

June 26th, 2008

A successful person enjoys a beautiful sunset and knows

somewhere that very same sun is dawning a new day.

Midnight

July 3rd, 2008

I killed you little kitty

I didn't mean to do it

I didn't see you 'Midnight', crouching in the road

A moments inattentiveness has caused my great forebode

How can I give this meaning when all I am is sad

How can I ask forgiveness when I feel so very bad

The answer is you gave so much and some might not have

noticed

But I am waking up and becoming better focused

For when I'm inattentive I create a great divide

yet you still gave a message to me just before you died

Grateful little 'Midnight' for your dear sacrifice

Sending me a message at the very dearest price

Save for you, I'll pay attention to the Ones I love tonight.

Wisdom

July 17th, 2008

The passing of years is no guarantee of Wisdom.

Wisdom comes to those who have experienced pain

and not allowed it to defeat them.

Voices

July 22nd, 2008

When I listen to the whispers of that still small voice,

there's less shouting later.

Forgiveness

July 23rd, 2008

Please forgive me.

Forgive me not for me, but for your Self.

Forgive me for all the wrongs I have done you.

Forgive me for deeds intentional and unintentional.

Forgive me for the little things and the big ones too.

Not because I need redemption but so you may live.

So you may live free.

Free of all the encumbrances

and bindings that resentment breeds.

So you may see your rainbows in vibrant colors,

not dull and muted tones.

Forgive me so you can live free

For although I would

give anything,

do anything,

be anything

to free you,

only you can free yourself.

If you ask me how I know this,

it's simple.

I know it by firsthand experience.

My freedom began the moment I forgave you.

Loving Now

August 7th, 2008

Death is inevitable

Death is as natural as birth and living

Death is a doorway we all shall pass through

Neither run from it, nor to it

For to do so takes attention

From the most precious thing there is

Now

Forever live in this most precious moment

With all your heart,

There is no other moment exactly like this one

There are an infinite number of moments

Each one unique and each one occurring

Now

Fear lives in the past

Fear lives in the future

Love lives Now

I Love

Now

Truth

August 18th, 2008

The only Truth I know

Is the Truth in my Heart

Truth cannot be explained

Please don't try

Truth cannot be 'learned'

Truth is felt

Truth is experienced, first hand

Truth is personal and is the one gift

that cannot be given away

You cannot give it to me and

I cannot give it to you

I must give it to my Self

Happiness

August 27th, 2008

Life is all illusion

It's not what you do

But how I perceive what you do

So in a sense I am responsible for what you do

Not in a real sense but in the sense that

The only thing that is real for me

Is my perception of your action

And I always always always

Have the freedom

To change my perception

That freedom is the key

The most miraculous key to

Happiness

Pressure

September 2nd, 2008

There is no such thing as external pressure

All pressure is internally created in my mind

This is both my prison and my ultimate escape

to freedom

Sailing the Sea of Life

September 20th, 2008

On the Sea of Life without a hand on the tiller

I drift at sea and may easily spend my entire life adrift.

To reach paradise is the goal, yet it is not the destination.

Paradise is achieved by the attempt,

by moving in the direction of the

unattainable perfection.

Spontaneity

September 20th, 2008

It seems I have great difficulty planning spontaneity.

Timeless

September 23rd, 2008

Remembering I was there

Aware I am here

Knowing I shall always Be

Ups and Downs

September 24th, 2008

As I descend down the slope into the depths of the valley

I gain momentum, energy and faith to climb the next hill

My Monster

September 28th, 2008

I have an ugly monster
It lives inside my head
It doesn't like to play real nice
Sometimes it wants me dead

But when I learn to love it,
yes, give it love and care
its little monster tendencies
just start to disappear

For when I learn to love it
and hold it in my arms
it isn't quite as scary
in fact I see its charms

It cannot harm me any more
I've learned how we can win
My monster is a part of me

And I am Whole again

Nature's Energy

September 30th, 2008

In the quiet of Nature, all is as it is

In the quiet of my Mind all is as it is

I feel the Energy of Nature

I feel the Energy of my Mind

And know there is no difference

Energy is God expressing

Choice

October 3rd, 2008

Perhaps my reason for being here

on Earth is to learn how to choose.

Instincts

October 6th, 2008

My mind thinks it knows so much

it thinks my animal instincts are beneath it

and yet I've never seen a worried songbird.

Where is When?

October 7th, 2008

When?

When is a question in the time domain

When can only be asked in the manifest world

In the Spiritual World there is no when

In Spirit the word when is as nebulous

as God is in the manifest world

Compassion

October 10th, 2008

Know there are Beings you have never met

who care about you,

beings who believe we belong to the same family,

the family of Self Aware Beings

Resentment

October 13th, 2008

Knowing that holding resentment is poison is not enough. Like any addiction the change for healing must be embodied deep within my heart for any lasting change to occur

Ego

October 14th, 2008

My ego thinks it is a monolith

A great and mighty mountain

It thinks it is the source of all

An endless bountiful fountain

But it has cracks where rain seeps in

Deep into the interior

And when attacked by wind and rain

It fears it is inferior

The Spirit of the water is deep

Harsh icy cold of winter comes

and the freezes hard within it

The mountain cracks wide open

and sheds its useless cover

Revealing a brand new shining face

And a chance to start all over

Evil

October 16th, 2008

When evil outside of me I see

and a wall I start to build

I create a separate entity

Where none exists but in my mind

There is no-thing out there to fear

For deep within we all are Kind

Patience

October 17th, 2008

To know and understand the onion

I peel it slowly layer by layer

letting each layer reveal itself to me.

If I try to rush and cut to the core with a sharp knife

I cause pain for the onion and tears for myself.

Onions and humans are not so different

Walls

October 20th, 2008

Who built this wall?

Was it you or was it me?

Or did we by mutual agreement

contribute stones together,

the one thing we worked so well at building

stone by stone over the years

until we talked over it

but no longer saw each other's face.

How long must I wait for you to look over

and see my tears for what I wish would be?

Then the lightning strikes me and I know

if I would but remove my stones the wall would fall

and I would clearly see you are no foe.

The Next Step

October 24th, 2008

Today I take that next step.

I take it like it is my very first

and I take it like it is my last.

There really is no difference.

The only step I can ever take is the next one.

I can't go back to undo the steps I took yesterday.

I can't know the steps I shall take tomorrow.

The only step that matters is the one I take today,

and so I take it with the enthusiasm of a child.

I take it boldly and with confidence

and know in my heart

it is the right step for me to take today.

Today I take that next step.

Reason and Love

October 26th, 2008

Awakening or enlightenment is the result

of rational thought powered by Love

Reason is the chisel in the hands of the sculptor

and Love, their Divine Desire to create

Judging

October 27th, 2008

In much of my life now

I have forgotten how to judge.

Perhaps this explains my last jury duty

There wasn't a single call for a jury panel all day.

Door to the Heart

October 28th, 2008

I now know the door to your heart opens outward.

Please forgive me for pushing so hard on it for so long.

Blue Marble

October 30th, 2008

Little Blue Marble spinning in the dark

How long will you spin?

A big question mark

What is your purpose?

Why are you here?

Do you hear Humanity?

Do you feel our fear?

Are you simply waiting?

For the explosion of Light

Forever increasing awareness of our improving sight

Critical mass is reached

We're not quite so dense

Humanity awakens to its own magnificence

Curiosity

October 31st, 2008

Love is expressed

by honest interest and curiosity in another.

So tell me please, what do you Love?

What fills your heart up to overflowing?

Tell me please, so I may be in Love.

Pressure

November 6th, 2008

Living with an open mind means there is little need to let off steam. Steam only builds pressure in a closed container

Infinity Up and Down

November 10th, 2008

And so I gaze at the spinning globe. I see what a precious jewel it is. I marvel at how much history is contained on that tiny sphere. And then I imagine that all the trillions of atoms in my body have as much or more history and so too the billions of galaxies beyond our own. An infinite number of micro and macro worlds. On into Infinity both up and down and I wonder in all those micro and macro worlds. How many other collections of Divine particles are able to contemplate their own existence?

Sound

November 11th, 2008

Today I say thank you for sound

The sound of Hummer mewing for his breakfast in the morning

The sound of cold wind whipping by my ears on a bike ride

The sound of birds chirping in the morning

The recorded sound of Karyn singing in my ear thirty years later

The sound of silence in my mind

The sound of engines roaring

The sound of frogs croaking in the water

The sound of crickets chirping in the night

The sound of a door, she knows the last child is home

The sound of my Mother's last words

'I see it . It's All clear to me now'

Oyster

December 6th, 2008

It's safe and comfortable inside my shell

Nothing can hurt me, all is well

My pearl is my treasure and I must protect it

If I open my shell others reject it

But why can't I see, it's so very dark

The light that's inside me refuses to spark

The carnivores out there disembowel me

I dare not open unless God has found me

But how can I know before I commit?

Where's my guarantee and how does it fit?

Where is the beauty when I live in the dark?

Where is the singing of the beautiful lark?

Without a risk nothing is gained

No man's an island I hear the refrain

So the answer is courage to be what I am

To open my shell and be like a lamb

To be open to slaughter and when I survive

I know in my heart that I'm truly alive!

Giving

December 10th, 2008

At Carl's Junior today I paid for the person behind on my dime

I haven't done that in a long time

And seeing now there's nothing wrong

I ask, why did I wait so long?

I also ask which came first, the Joy or the Giving.

Ah yes, a circle, has no beginning and no ending

Turning Around

December 18th, 2008

When I turn my back on my gorilla

pretending he isn't there,

he is the monkey on my back

following everywhere I go

and the fear of attack consumes my attention

and diverts the energy flow from the Divine

Yet, when I turn and face him

I find the monkey is dancing and I'm the organ grinder.

And I need only find a tune he can dance to

Thorns and Petals

December 19th, 2008

Today a new rose bud appears at the darkest point in winter

I cherish it and nurture it and give it water and light and care.

Though at this time I see mostly thorns I know they too

are as much an attribute of its beauty as its soft velvet petals.

I give thanks for the blessing of the entire rose,

thorns and petals

Equality

January 4th, 2009

When a child looks up to me

May I see her without looking down

The Leap

January 6th, 2009

I stand, my back to the sheer granite face

My feet on the ledge of the human race

I face the Infinite Darkness below

I hear the raging waters flow

I am so cold in the freezing rain

I want no more to feel this pain

I slip on the crumbling rock at my feet

Afraid of the fate I'm about to meet

Soon I shall slip into the abyss

saddened by all the sweet kisses I'll miss

I am so frightened of the fall

And yet . . . I leap and give up my all

I waited so long and now wonder why

when inside me I knew all along

I can fly

No Looking Back

January 7th, 2009

Airplanes have no rear windows.

When moving forward at high speed

there is no need to look back.

Oneness

January 21st, 2009

When the crash of thunder no longer startles me

I know I am grounded in my truth.

When I see the Light from above on a cloudy day

I know I am no longer a slave to my conditions.

When I can be Love in the face of scorn and betrayal

then I am fully aware of Oneness.

Nothing, Everything and Love

January 29th, 2009

I have nothing

All my efforts have been for naught

All my saving, and scrimping

All my striving for stuff

All my working for knowledge

No matter how much I succeed it shall never be enough

All of it is of no consequence.

It is all a dream

It is all a magnificent and exciting roller coaster ride

I have struggled so long to get everything

only to find I am climbing an infinite vertical rock face

I shall never reach the top

At the end I have the same as at the start

which is nothing

absolutely nothing,

nothing but Love

and that of course is

Everything

Everything with Nothing

February 9th, 2009

I can fly without wings

I can sing without voice

I can be nourished without food

I can walk without legs

I can hug without arms

I can touch without skin

I can see without eyes

I can dance without feet

I can give without wealth

I can receive without taking

I can cry without tears

I can succeed without approval

I can love without need

I can do Everything with Nothing

With Love I can do anything and everything

I always have Love in Infinite Supply

I am connected to the Source of Infinite Love

I can give Love for all eternity

For that is the meaning of Infinity

Love and Fear, Darkness and Light

February 8th, 2009

You live in your fear and I live in mine

Both fearful to truly let our Light shine

Were I to trust and share the deepest me

would you run to hide fearing to be free?

Or invite the monster into the Light

And hug it there in plain sight?

And whether you choose Love or fear

would I choose Love and be of good cheer

Dare I take the leap into the unknown

to stare down the darkness all alone?

Knowing the Light comes from within

Knowing with Self Love we always win

Judgment

February 14th, 2009

When I choose to judge you to your face

and in my righteousness put you in your place.

I stand on the precipice holding a knife.

Creating a world of misery and strife.

I want you to love me in the end,

but think my hate can cause me to win.

Yet my judgment of you is a double edged sword

It cuts you to the quick but also the cord.

It keeps us separate in our own small space.

When God only knows there's only One Face.

For my judgment of you I only can see,

when the monster in you is also in me.

So from this day forward I choose to be free.

To recognize everyone's on God's Tree

With malice towards none and freedom for all,

I let my Light shine and knock down that wall.

Miracle of Life

February 19th, 2009

Where I am going I must go alone.

You cannot come with me.

Like the butterfly or baby chick

I must break free of the darkness on my own

to gain the strength I require

for the next leg of my journey.

I must learn to lean only on myself.

Only in self-reliance shall I grow to embrace you freely.

Only in standing on my own shall I be free to stand with you.

So do not follow me, but look for your own dream

and should we find each other still

that shall be the expression of True Love.

The Road Ahead

February 23rd, 2009

When the road is before me

And I know it is my road,

yet the fear is welling up and urging me to turn back,

I kindly embrace my ego and tell it

all is well.

This is our journey.

This is the road to Peace.

This is road to Health.

This is the road to Light.

and fear is to be expected.

For courage is only possible in the presence of fear

and growth is only possible with courage.

Now is the time for growth, courage and the loving embrace of

the Unknown.

This is the road to Freedom.

In this moment I take the first step down the road.

All is well.

Love and Fear

February 24th, 2009

Fear lives in the past.

Fear lives in the future.

Love is always Now.

Do Not Follow

February 25th, 2009

When I see my path clearly,

I have no need for you to follow me.

I do not seek your approval.

My Truth is for me and I cannot give it to you.

You shall find your truth in your own place and time.

This is the way of it.

This is how it has always been

from the moment the first person said

I am.

Breakthrough

February 28th, 2009

The breakthrough occurs

when I bring the outside in

and turn my inside out.

When you are no longer out there.

When my heart has grown three sizes this day

and I cry for all that I have done to you

in my thoughts

then the walls come crumbling down

and I am Love.

I am Peace.

I am Joy.

I am Beautiful,

and so are you,

because we are One.

Turning Back

March 2nd, 2009

When distractions take my attention from You

I notice, and gently turn back to face You.

You look into my soul with love and compassion

as if I never left.

This is what is meant by practice.

My heart knows You cannot leave me.

You are there in my darkest of nights.

You are there in my brightest of days.

You are there when my eyes are closed.

You are there when I am cursing the world.

You are there when I am praising It too.

You are All Knowledge,

All Power

All Presence

You are God

and we are One.

Ready

March 3rd, 2009

How can I know if I am ready?

What signs will I see?

Fear is present so I can be brave.

Uncertainty is present so I can explore the Unknown.

Friends are present to encourage me.

Faith is present so I know what commitment feels like.

Expectation is here so I may create my dream.

Love is present, always.

I am Love.

It is time.

I am ready.

I'm waiting on nothing Now.

Joyful Noise

March 6th, 2009

Let the celebration begin.

Let the fireworks commence.

Let all the stops be pulled out.

Let Joy explode from the depths of being.

Let Nature shout to the Heavens above.

Let Nothing be held back.

Let all that is express fully and with Infinite Enthusiasm.

Let me see God in All of it.

Why?

For no reason at all.

Joy defies all reason.

Truth and Fear

March 7th, 2009

Why do I fear the truth?

Why does the lie seem so comfortable

when it feels like hiding a porcupine in my pants?

Why am I afraid to see what my heart knows

Why do I choose the sidelines

safe and protected from the risks of Life

but missing the Euphoria

God give me courage to be honest

with my Self

Friend

March 9th, 2009

You are my Friend.

I know this is true

for though I share my deepest thoughts

and the world does not agree

you do not judge me.

You understand the importance of Trust.

You give without need for response.

You know the true meaning of Love

and by your knowing

I know it too.

The gift you give is great

for now I understand

Love and non-judgment are one in the same.

Thank you my friend

To Be

March 10th, 2009

Today I choose not to resist.

Today I have no need to persist.

I am water flowing over rocks/

My Life is new and it talks.

I am feeling and I am fine

for this is my touching of the Divine.

I am Wind, Rain, Sea, Sky and Me.

I am here simply to be

Walking Awhile

March 11th, 2009

Would you like to walk with me awhile?

Please do not come if you need me.

Do not come if you think I need you.

Do not come to teach me.

Do not come to be taught.

Come if your heart is in it.

Come because you are my friend.

Come not because we are 'in love'.

Come because each of us is Love.

Come because I am your friend.

Requirements

March 12th, 2009

There really are no requirements for my Life,

unless I create them or re-create them.

I Am Free

March 20th, 2009

I am free to have intimate conversations

in total silence without fear.

Walking in Silence

March 24th, 2009

We met today for the first time

and walked together in silence.

We are family.

I trust you for the gift you bring me.

The gift of sharing this moment,

together.

We have no past and no expectation of future.

We share now with a Love so deep

there is no longing.

Simply a willingness to walk together

until our paths diverge.

This is Love

this is what we are.

Infinite Space

April 2nd 2009

When I ask a question

and you do not answer.

I realize that silence is an answer.

In Emptiness there is Space.

In Space there is Silence.

In Silence there is Infinity.

In Infinity there is Freedom.

Morning Walk

April 10th, 2009

Walking in silence in the morning mist

I am God naming things, making a list

Horses, trails, flowers and trees

Roses and weeds and buzzing bees

Humming birds and mud on my shoes

Morning papers showing the news

Whoops, that's a story just give it a name

Paper and words, pictures of flame

The setting full Moon and the morning star

All things I've seen and now they just are

Seeing it all as neither bad or good

Getting lost inside my own neighborhood

Losing my thoughts losing my "mine"

Knowing for certain the Universe is kind

It's been there all along for me to see

and now it is different

It reflects me

I Am Okay

April 11th, 2009

Hugging the monster in plain sight

To walk into hell in spite of my fright

That's when I grow

That's when I know

I am okay

Letting Go Honestly

April 18th, 2009

Today my world changed

I gave up something I thought so important,

something I had held so tight

It was squishing out between my fingers.

Then I just let it go.

I choose to be in my business for once.

I chose the path I knew would upset another,

and lo they welcomed it with gratitude.

My enemy was me, only me.

My God, I'm alive again.

The world changed.

The sun came out again,

or was it just me

waking up from a deep sleep?

Seeing clearly, honestly, authentically,

knowing who I am

and being comfortable with my Self,

knowing I am enough.

Empty Space

April 29th, 2009

I am up before the sun.

Let it find me having fun.

Let it be just what it is

without a thought of mine or his.

Let me take this day for me

and give it to Eternity!

So as the day puts forth its wonders,

do I watch or do I plunder?

Or do I release the deeper Self

For more to see and know my health

For when I share I open doors

And a vast and Empty Space is yours!

Time Is My Friend

May 1st, 2009

The Universe does not rush or delay. The Universe unfolds with perfect timing. It knows when each step of the evolving emergence of Creation is to manifest and it does it with ease and Grace. The Divine Plan has a completely harmonious relationship with time. There is no struggle, no need to hurry or waste time waiting. Each step knows its time is to appear. This is the Nature of the Universe. This is the Nature of God. This is my Nature.

I have a loving and harmonious relationship with time. I am a Wizard of Time and Space and time is my friend. When I live each moment as the most important moment of my life I experience an Aliveness that is indescribable. For this moment is truly the only moment I ever have. Knowing that I am immortal now and always I choose to live every moment fully.

When I am friendly to this moment this moment is friendly to me. I choose to be positive no matter what the apparent condition that presents itself. I see beyond the physical condition and know that my perception can and does change my reality and the world. For this knowledge I am fully grateful. I bless this moment and release it for a free exchange of energy with the Divine perfectly unfolding Universe. Thank you God! And So It Is

Joy

May 1st, 2009

I am ready to fly solo,

to soar on the winds,

to fly without fear of falling,

to be dependent on no one and no thing,

to know I am nothing and everything

and be okay with it,

to speak my truth gently with authenticity,

kindness and understanding,

to take off the mask and see clearly in the mirror

the beauty and the ugliness

and not have a preference.

I have no need to fix ugliness.

I have no need to fixate on beauty.

All that Spirit brings me is a Gift.

Joy!

The Joy of Detachment

May 16th, 2009

I see possibilities

where there were none.

Without effort it can be fun.

Sitting with presence;

No need for the doing.

All is fulfilled and I am renewing.

I can be present and not feel your pain.

I can be with you and not need you sane.

Mad as a hatter and still in my mind.

Sane is a story, important is kind.

Be what I am and let you be you

and when we're together

that's beautiful too.

No more neediness.

No more approval.

No longer a victim requiring removal.

You are a gift and so am I,

apart or together I know we shall fly!

A Rare Bird

May 24th, 2009

I am up once more before the sun.

Seeing Joy in everyone.

Loving you and loving me.

I know in my heart I am free.

Loving what is, is where it's at.

Not needing it this way not needing it that.

I'm grateful for you, I'm grateful for me.

I'm grateful that courage brings me such glee!

So like a bird I spread my wings

and into my life a rare songbird sings!

Running Away

June 17th, 2009

Why am I running?

Where am I running?

Am I running up?

Or am I running down?

Am I running from or am I running to?

What fear causes me to run to or from you?

Am I lost on the path or finding my way,

Am I running to me or going astray?

I look in your eyes and I run into my Self.

I used to run, to embrace the One.

But racing pell-mell wasn't much fun.

I missed all the flowers on the way.

Now I walk and see things each day.

No need to run no need to race

once I'm aware God's every place.

Toast of BegEnding

June 20th, 2009

May the Love you have shared

not be compared.

May it grow throughout the seasons

and bring you Joy without reasons.

May it carry you through the challenges ahead.

May it be the guiding light on your path

throughout your lives together.

Here's to a new BegEnding!

Knowing No's

June 25th, 2009

When is saying **no**, a **yes**?

When it's honest to my Self.

When is saying **yes** a **no**?

When I am answering to please you

then I am lying to myself.

I am hiding me in fear of your rejection,

when deep within I know rejection does not exist.

For rejection is just another form of Love.

It gives me what I need to grow and expects no reward.

Unconditional giving is how I receive.

How do I know when my **no** is honest

and when it is running away?

When my heart feels no pain in the action,

when my **no** is said with Love in my heart,

when my **no** has **no** attachment,

then my **no** is a **yes** to me!

No Place To Know

June 27th, 2009

How many days does it take

to reach enlightenment?

How many years?

How many centuries?

How many lifetimes?

But the sage says,

"You ask the wrong question."

Enlightenment is not in time.

Enlightenment is transcendent.

It cannot be found.

It cannot even be searched for.

It cannot be grasped.

Truth is beyond dreams and things and even thinking.

As soon as I think the thought I'm enlightened

I'm in illusion again.

Beyond thoughts of you and I and the world

is that place of nothingness.

That place where I have nothing to hang onto.

Forever falling into the abyss

I was there briefly once in my youth

It frightened me and I came back,

back to the known real world,

back to the illusion.

I have believed the illusion for a brief moment now,

forty years or so.

Now I desire with all my heart to return

to no place to know.

Still, I ask the wrong question

with the paradigm of time and space.

I cannot escape into the sublime nothingness

by 'doing' in the real world

or even by thinking.

Thinking creates the illusion and the lies,

lies I tell myself to make myself comfortable and sane.

Yet there is no comfort or sanity in lies.

The truth lies in the no mind,

in the non-knowing,

in Being

In free falling without fear of the inevitable ground.

WEEEEeeeeeeeeee!

What Is a Friend?

August 20th, 2009

What is a friend?

Can I be your friend without you being mine?

Can I be your friend without telling you?

Can I still be your friend if you unfriend me?

Can I still see the face of God when you are unfriendly?

Can you really be unfriendly or is it only my story that you are?

If you are unfriendly am I responsible for how you see me?

Where does my responsibility for your happiness begin?

And where does it end?

Must I see through your eyes to be your friend?

Must I be with you in some sense to truly be your friend?

If I choose not to know your heart can I ever truly know mine?

Arrogance

September 4th, 2009

Arrogance is the wall I create between us.

My armor and protection to keep me safe.

Is it True? What is safety?

Can I be safe inside this shell

that keeps me separate from you?

God let me walk naked through the battlefield

shells bursting all around bullets flying

without fear of the pain you can give me.

Let me see that pain as your gift.

God let me cry for you and know I am crying for myself

God let me live! Yes God let me live ... again

for the first time

connected with all that is.

Connected to you

Breathing

September 5th, 2009

Who am I?

When I've let go of everything

who am I?

No possessions, no job,

no family, no thoughts

What is left?

Emptiness

The vast Void

Infinite open Space

And I am still breathing

When I breathe this body

who is breathing?

Can I choose not to breathe?

Something is breathing me

What is that?

Spiraling into Infinity

September 6th, 2009

How far can I go?

Is there any limit

to my consciousness?

How deep is deep?

How high is the sky?

The spiral gets faster,

as I ascend it

level upon level

higher and higher

There is no top

There is no end

Just 'BegEnding' upon 'BegEnding'

You become a blur as

the frequency increases

I begin to spin

into Me

into You

into Infinity

Up Again

October 13th, 2009

I'm up before six, isn't it great?

I'm up before six no need to wait

I'm up before six and ready for doing

I'm up before six and know I'm just Being

All is ok, even when it's not

Everything I fear is only a thought!

Thank you Katie for helping me see

Thank you me for showing me, Me!

Tell the Truth

December 16th, 2009

Tell the truth

Tell it now

Tell the truth

Don't worry 'bout how

Tell the truth

Don't try to protect me

Tell the truth

It can no longer reject me

Tell the truth

I really want to know

Tell me your thoughts

Without the fear I may go

Tell the truth

I promise to listen

Tell the truth

So there's nothing I'm miss'n

Tell the truth

I am ready now to hear it

Tell the truth

I no longer fear it

Tell the truth

Before it's too late

Tell the truth

I simply can't wait

I've taught you so well to tell me lies

I'm ready now for *The Lord of the Flies*

The truth is kind

The truth is Love

The truth is my savior

The truth is my dove

The truth brings me Peace

For all of it's good

Even the bad stuff

Especially the bad stuff

Grateful

Feeling Words

February 4th, 2010

How can I convey deep feelings to you with words?

When all that I see is through a veil

The glass between us is smoky

I see you as the other, indistinctly

I see the shadow you cast and think that is you

I create myths and stories to convince myself I know

I think I know you

yet I know nothing of you

and then I decide to look within

and deep within myself I am surprised to see

You

We are One

Letting Lose

February 5th, 2010

Why must I win?

What drives me to beat you?

My friend the ego and his need to be right

and when I win and you are defeated

Have I won

or have I in some sense lost all hope?

Have I separated us into neat and organized piles of

winners and losers

Have I created an enemy, resentment and pain

that one day rises up and knocks me off my pile?

All victories are temporal.

All triumphs are fleeting.

How can I do this differently?

How can I let you win and not see myself as losing?

How indeed?

Trust for No Reason

February 11th, 2010

It is said that trust must be earned

and that is not my experience

when I give trust freely for no earthly reason

it inspires others to go beyond their own limits

and manifest miracles.

Natural Balance

February 16th, 2010

Nature is the fulcrum on which all Life balances.
Natural Law is always moving to balance the excesses and the
scarcities.
In silence I become attune to sound.
In anger I search for peace.
In my shallowness I yearn for depth.
From my depth I learn to be light hearted again.
In my dark prison I find the crack in the dungeon wall
and see the Light streaming into my soul.
I welcome this balance.
I recognize this balance as Nature.
I recognize this balance as God.
I welcome the dark moments for they never come alone.
As Emerson says in every wounded oyster there is a pearl.
I know it is all good.
I know to be grateful for being awakened from a comfortable
sound sleep.
It speaks to me of a new adventure, calling me.
I choose to answer the call.
It is all for me.
It is all for God.

Being God

Last night I heard someone tell about a student of New Thought speaking to Ram Das about having parents with more traditional religious beliefs. When Ram Das asked him how he dealt with his parents he said, "They don't have an issue when I am being God, it's only when I talk about it."

I have said enough for today.

I Appreciate You

February 18th, 2010

I appreciate you

In countless ways, so let me count up to infinity

When you see something from a whole new angle

That I never saw before

When you live your life as you believe

When you do something that brings you joy

When you listen to me

When I listen to you

I appreciate you for telling me your mind

And for not always agreeing with me

I appreciate that you let me make mistakes

And I appreciate when you tell me about them

I appreciate your intelligence

I appreciate your caring for others

Your love of animals

I appreciate your willingness to walk into the fire

Your courage to walk your own path

That you don't need to follow the pack

I appreciate your uniqueness

Your kindness

Your calmness

I appreciate that you care enough to connect

I appreciate your intense enthusiasm for all that you love

I appreciate your commitment

I appreciate your gifts

Most simply

I appreciate your Love

In all the myriad of ways you express it

I Love you

Today's To-Do List

February 19th, 2010

Be

Simply Love

February 20th, 2010

Have a ball

Run like the wind

Fly like the eagle

Soar to heights never thought possible

Love

Simply Love and all is given

Want Confusion

March 3rd, 2010

What you want confuses me

Though I try to give it to you, I fail

Why is that, do you think?

Why is that, do I think?

Because I'm needing you to receive it

It isn't for your needs

It's for mine

I need you to have what you want

So I can be happy

When I can give you what you want

with a Love so deep that I care not if you receive my gift

I am Love

Receiving Good

March 4th, 2009

As I start this day I see the presence and perfection of God in everything. Everywhere, everything, everyone is Divine. I see the face of God. I know beauty, love, kindness, peace, wisdom, joy, light, grace, power and enthusiasm expresses in all that I see. There is good for me and I know, yes I know it is mine.

I too experience all the attributes of God, for I am an individual expression of the One. I rejoice in this knowledge. I am excited about Life. I am filled up to overflowing with gratitude for every experience. It is all good, even the bad stuff; Especially the bad stuff. There is no bad stuff. It's like the warning track in baseball telling me of the nearness of the wall, gifting me with information that I use for my Good. There is the peace that surpasses all understanding. I have work that I love! I clearly see the next step to achieve my dreams. I am a skillful communicator. I speak with confidence. I encourage others today.

With childlike innocence I venture forth into the world with no agenda for the way it should be. I know that "what is", is best. I Love what is. I know that my good surrounds me and I have fun and play with every experience. I know that in playing the game of Life I learn and I grow. I play and turn "have to" into "get to"!

I feel the joy of knowing my good is present and I am in a continual state of gratitude for my good. And so it is!

The Miracle in Me

March 5th, 2010

So long I tried to fix them

To teach them

To help them

To be kinder to them

To show them the way

To be the example so they would learn

I was the blind man holding elephant's tail

Certain it was a rope

I deceived myself thinking I was better

That I wanted the best for them

While all along they could see

What I wanted was the best for me

Then one day I began to see

The only one to work was me

And so I answered the call

I left my home and family

Left all that I knew

And in that far off land I found something new

I discovered my Self

And when I returned they were different

They were perfect, whole and complete

No fixing required

Imagine that

Yes I did

Independent Balance

September 7th; 2011

Where is the balance between autonomy and connection? Where is the balance between independence and communion? How do I recognize I am one with you and all things and not lose myself?

While I fear losing myself can I ever hope to find myself? Where is the emptiness that I can hold on to? Where is the fullness I can let go of? How can I hear your desires, wants and needs without giving up mine? Without giving up me. How much of me shall I give up to you? How much of me am I giving up to God? Where is the balance between autonomy and connection? Where is the balance between independence and communion?

How much shall I Love?

I Move

September 9th, 2011

From a place of serenity I recognize the unimaginable magnificence of this world. I recognize that all is here for my Good. I recognize that I am the creator of my Good.

I no longer sit idly by waiting. I move. I choose a direction. I focus on my Good. I am now discerning. I am now confident in my direction. I am not deterred by circumstance. I am peacefully certain of my place. I am willing to participate. I am willing to fail. I am willing to succeed.

Knowing that neither success nor failure is my master. I am aware that my work is to direct my life. My work is to focus my attention on a feeling of wholeness. I focus now. I know I am captain of my ship. I am able to direct my thoughts attention and energy in the direction of my dreams, and Joy presents itself the moment I commit. So I swing wide the doors to my heart, my mind and move forward undeterred by what appears as obstacles. Every rock I step over or around strengthens me.

I am Power and Presence and Knowledge expressing in through and AS God. Nothing can stop me now. For I know how to direct my thoughts and thus I know how my thoughts create my feelings and I absolutely know that where I have deep emotions and feelings my world reflects those right back to me.

So I move. I move to Joy. I move to enthusiasm. I move in the direction of my increasing good on the spiral up into my amazing Life.

Grateful for this feeling which I know has all the power of the Universe within it, I release and let go and know, truly know . . . It is done!

What I Imagine

September 11th, 2011

I imagine a day when

instead of never forgetting

we remember to remember

We remember that we all are brothers and sisters

We remember that every act of violence

was begot by an act that preceded it

We remember that when we allow fear

to control our actions

we open the door to our own terror

We remember that a world of love doesn't just mean

my family

my tribe

my country

my race

but the entire planet,

the entire Universe

I imagine a day when we know

that when we allow ourselves to hate another,

when we cannot see through their eyes,

we have ourselves become what we are fighting

I imagine a day when

we remember to see an act of violence as a cry for Love,

when we remember that there are no mistakes

We remember that truly what we are, in essence,

cannot be harmed

I imagine a day when we lead with Love,

Love for our similarities and our differences

I imagine that day is Today

Two Songs
Harmony within Discord

September 16th, 2011

Where is the illusive Light?

Where is the laughter?

Where is the infinite Love I seek?

I hear two songs playing together

They are not in tune

Is it my business to orchestrate them?

Or to turn one off and play only the other?

Now one is louder

It drowns out the other song

Yet I know it is still there

Now and then I hear a discordant note coming through

And when I'm quiet I hear the other

How can I hear them both playing together?

Am I the composer, conductor or the audience?

And still the two songs play simultaneously in my head

Can I hear harmony within discord?

Can I appreciate them both without needing to quiet one?

Can I know that each has Love in it?

Each playing from its highest place

Each expressing the God within

Can I be clear as to my place in each song

Crystal clear in my purpose

Knowing I am here for both songs

Knowing I can love them both

Knowing I can love the independence of each

The different tempo

The different style

The different mood

Knowing that each can change in a moment

And can I still love the change

Knowing that each has something to offer me

Accepting both gifts

Love and Law

Everything I Need Is within Me Now

June 28th, 2013

I recognize the infinite power of God in, through and as all that there is. Everything seen and everything un-scene is all God. God's power is unlimited. God's knowledge is infinite. God is everywhere. So God is right here where I am. Now! Knowing that everything is God, that includes me. I am that same perfect individualized cosmic self that I came here to be when I was born and I am here to express my Divinity. The God-self within me expresses in this and every moment. I am God's unique expression of Jon as God. All that I need is within me Now because God expresses in through and as me. I welcome support from others but my ultimate source of all that I require comes from the God within me expressing vibrantly, joyously and with Love.

I greet this day with enthusiasm knowing it is already a tremendous success. I cannot fail for I recognize now that any apparent setback is simply a detour sign showing me another path up the mountain. Arrival at the top is assured. I know the way because God expresses AS me. The Light shines and guides me at each step.

I am ever grateful to know my divinity and oneness with it all. Knowing it is already done, I release my word into the Law which takes care of how. It is done. Ashe.

Up on Top before the Sun

June 30th, 2013

I am seeing God in everything and everyone. The infinite power is right here and now. No need to question why or how. There is a power greater than I and I can use it to reach for the sky. It can heal all ills it can make me grow. It has all the knowledge I'll ever need to know. I know I am one with all that there is.

In this sacred moment of grace I open myself up to hearing in this place. I welcome this day and the suns golden rays.

I'm grateful for all that I give and receive and release my word to Law with joyous God's speed. And so it is

I Love Myself and I Am Enough

July 1st, 2013

There is One Power in this Universe. It is unbounded. It is unlimited. It is the Power that creates everything. And this One Power is right here where I am now. I am one with this Infinite Power. I direct it for my good.

There is good for me and I am open and receptive to receiving it now. All apparent negative conditions are simply appearances and change the moment I know the truth. I declare the truth now that I am healthy, confident and filled with love and joy for life with a deep knowing that I am enough. I choose to love myself from the inside out. All that I need or want is right here within me now because God is within me now and always and God is infinite Love.

I am grateful for all the blessings in my life in the form of people, experiences, community and abundant loving relationships. I release this into the Law knowing it is done. And so it is

Choice is My Greatest Gift

July 3rd, 2013

I recognize that Infinite Power that is all, does all, creates all, knows all and is ever present. Further I know that this Power is within me now. This Power is in this place the wisdom of all of the Universe is available to me right now right where I am. This is because this Power is one with me and I am one with it. God in through and as me is expressing Divinity in every moment of every day.

I recognize that my greatest gift is my ability to choose. I choose in this moment to align myself with the harmony and nature of God and to move along that path which aligns myself with the flow of the Divinity of the Universe. I let go and I let God express through me now. I release attachments to specific outcomes knowing that every experience moves me along my right and perfect path. My Life is unfolding perfectly. The top of the mountain is assured and all is well, knowing that God expressing through me is perfection.

Grateful for knowing I am ever in God's grace, I feel great gratitude for this knowing. I am in my Divine right place and grateful for it. I now release this into the Law knowing it is done. And so it is.

Each Day I Grow More Resilient

July 4th, 2013

In this moment of deep inner silence from the top of my mountain I know Spirit is present here because Spirit is present everywhere. Spirit is beyond time and space. Spirit is simply all there is. I relax into this feeling of the all knowingness, infinite power and ever presence of Spirit. I let Spirit have its way with me. I feel it expressing in me, through me, as me and it feels right and healthy. I am whole and in that feeling of communion with Spirit I know the joy of Oneness. I know the peace of surrender. I know the Love of God.

This Love surrounds me. It strengthens me. Each day I grow in resilience, because I know a Love that cannot be diminished. It is the very nature of Reality. It is the nature of God. Love is God and God is Love. My choices are clear because my knowing comes from the Infinite knowing of Spirit and Spirit knows all that has ever been, all that there is, and all that will ever be. So I move into this day knowing that each choice is divinely guided. Knowing that I am in harmonic frequency with all there is and simply cannot make a mistake.

I have great gratitude for my knowing God is expressing as me. I release my word into the Law. And so it is

Today I Give My Gift

July 5th, 2013

Everything is God. God is the ultimate gift. The nature of God is to give unto itself. God expresses through each individualized being giving and receiving from each in an ever flowing continuous circulation of Good and that includes me. I am one with this Good for I am one with God.

Today I choose to give my gift knowing that my Life expands when I participate in the Divine Circulation of Good. I move past my fear of withholding into that space of conscious giving knowing that it is my Divine Nature to give and further knowing that as I give my gift it is the divine nature of the Universe that it returns to me multiplied abundantly. I welcome this expansion of my Life here today in this moment. I let my creativity expand and give my gift with great joy.

With tremendous gratitude for the gifts I have to give I released my word into the Law knowing it is done. And so it is.

Breath Supports Me

July 6th, 2013

I recognize the Breath of Spirit flowing in and out and through all that I see and all that is invisible to my eyes. This is the Energy of God moving through Everything. It is all Powerful, it is ever present and it is all knowing. It delivers to each individualized expression exactly what it needs in exactly right time in exactly the way that is needed. I recognize my own breath is coming into me from the Divine Source within me. I am one with the Breath of the Universe and the Breath of the Universe is one with me.

I breathe it in. I breathe it out. I feel the comfort of the Breath of the Universe. I feel the Power of the Breath of the Universe. I feel the security of the Breath of the Universe. I feel confidence in knowing It provides me all that I need. Breath supports me in every way possible. I am breathed and I am whole.

Grateful for Breath and for my knowing of its Power and Presence, I release my word into the Law with confidence, knowing all is well. Knowing it is done. And so it is.

I Relax and Feel God's Presence

July 8th, 2013

In this moment I relax, feeling and knowing God's ever present support. I am aware that God is Infinite Source. The flow of God's Love can never be diminished. It flows freely and effortlessly to and from everything there is. God is all there is. I feel it flowing through me. I relax my body and experience peace and confidence in knowing God is ever present in me. I am one with all that is and fully supported by all of it.

There is nothing that can separate me from God because Oneness is simply the nature of Reality. I now move into this day with confidence. Fear is met with Love and fades into nothingness just like turning on the light in the dark. My choices are clear. I know what is mine to do and I do it with new found Joy.

I am grateful to know I am always supported. I feel a calm confidence and give thanks for it. Knowing all this was already true before these words were spoken, I release my word into the Law. And so it is.

Fear Is My Path to Courage

July 10th, 2013

Even in the presence of fear I know God is ever present. God is the entirety of being. God is everywhere, in everything and everybody. God is in me now and always.

I recognize my fear as my path to wholeness. I know without fear there can be no courage so I embrace my fear and I accept my courageous path now. I know that courage comes not from me but from God manifesting in through and as me. Courage is ever available and I call on it now.

Grateful for my courage I move into this day knowing that fear is my friend when I recognize it as an opportunity for courageous forward movement on my path.

I release my word onto the Law knowing it is done. And so it is.

Today Is a New BegEnding

July 11th, 2013

I recognize God's presence in the Universe and in through and as me. God is in this place and I am one with all of it. I feel the Energy of God coursing through my body. All is working together for Good. I am powerful for my power comes from the One. I am wise for my wisdom comes from Universal Intelligence.

All movement is on the upward spiral moving me further along my perfect life path. All thoughts of retreat are now vanquished for now that I know the truth I can't go back to what I used to do. So I welcome this day with a new receptivity. I open my arms with Joy. There is Joy in my heart and lightness in my step. I see what is in front of me. I know what is mine to do and I do it. I release the old ways like taking off an old worn out coat that no longer protects me. I need no protection in God. I see and hear with new senses and I listen with my heart to the voice within.

My Life is unfolding perfectly and I am ever grateful for every lesson, treasured jewel, signpost and bump along the way. I release my word into the Law knowing all is well. Knowing it is done. And so it is.

Just Keep Swimming

July 13th, 2013

God is here right where I am. In the midst of all the feelings and emotions God's presence and Infinite Love cannot be avoided and I recognize it now. It is ever present. It is expressing itself through me. I am the vehicle for God's expression of Life. I am here for that expression to be manifest as me.

Today I consciously choose to release attachment to past concepts of how that expression should look. I embrace a new paradigm and trust the process and with that trust I just keep swimming. With Spiritual Principles as my guiding light, I know that all other concerns and conditions shall follow the light of principle based choices. I focus my attention at depth on who I now choose to be. I have new understanding of the importance of where I put my attention and am grateful for it.

With gratitude and confidence knowing that my words are simply a revealing and recognition of what is already so I release my word into the Law knowing it is done. And so it is..

My Most Conscious Relationship Is God

July 13th, 2013

Right now I recognize God is the ultimate relationship. God is in this very room. God is every room. God is in everyplace throughout this vast Universe. Everything is God. God is in through and expressing as each one present here this morning.

Today I am open and receptive to the exploration of conscious relationships. I know that every one of my relationships and the relationships of every person in this room is ultimately a Divine relationship with God. When I know that God is all there is, it is clear that in each and every relationship God is speaking to God because there is only one of us here. So every relationship is the Divine Expression of a sacred trust. I declare my receptivity right now to the deepening of my understanding of relationship and I recognize the potential for each person here to experience conscious relationships that enrich their lives. Today I choose to move beyond the shallow waters to depths where connection of loving hearts and open minds is a rich and satisfying experience.

Knowing spiritual growth is all about conscious relationship I welcome today's service with open arms. Grateful for today's opportunity to grow my relationships, I release my word into the Law knowing it is done and so it is.

I Proactively Choose to Grow

July 15th, 2013

The Power of God is Infinite. The intelligence of God is all knowing. The presence of God is everywhere. I recognize the Divine Urge to grow and express as a unique individualized expressions of God. I am an individualized expression with access to all the Power, Presence and Intelligence of God. I am one with all that is.

I draw from the Infinite Storehouse. I am proactive in my Life. I now choose to take positive steps towards my own growth. I know that I am fully supported by Spirit through which I live and move and have my being. All is working together in harmony for my growth. I welcome this growth into my Life. I recognize new found courage for moving through challenges. I now know that these challenges are not blocks but stepping stones up to the next level of my growth. I am ready willing and able to grow. All that I need is right here within me now because I know I am one with all that is.

I am grateful for my ability to choose to grow in response to the challenges I experience. I am grateful for my growth. I am grateful for the blessings in my Life. I release my word into the Law knowing it is done. And so it is.

I Am Whole

July 18th, 2013

I open wide to the recognition of God's presence. I feel the infinite power coursing through everything. I recognize I am one with all that is.

Grateful for this moment i release my word into the Law. And so it is.

Sleeping on an Elephant

September 6th, 2013

I wonder what it is like to sleep on the side of an elephant laying in shallow water. To feel the breath of her massive chest lifting me up and down. To feel the vibration of life as the air enters her great and powerful lungs. To lay there atop this magnificent creature and imagine what it is like to be her. What must it be like to have a trunk instead of hands to explore the world, to be able to breathe while swimming underwater, to have four legs, to have skin an inch thick, to have the ground shake when you run, to sleep with one eye open? I want to find my Elephant and read to her from the book of Life

Turning Away

September 7th, 2013

Turning her back on the past behind her

Facing what lies ahead knowing that God

as Spirit, Mind and Body is every present

like powerful elephants covering her back

No holding back for she is ever supported

Surrounded by water

Consciousness

Knowing

Being

Bird Path

September 8th, 2013

She is flying the bird path

One with the great bird above they soar

Together

Feeling the air

The lightness of feathers

Moving in unity with the wind

Flight and dance become one motion

Moving freely into Life

I want to dance my Bird Path and fly

I want to feel as the bird in flight

Bowing

September 10th, 2013

Bowing to the bird within

Captive for too long

Knowing that it longs to soar

She flies with it in unity of Spirit

Synchronized motion

With eyes the appearance of two

Close them and feel

The heart knows only One

One Life, grounded and in the air

Soaring

Joy Where Have You Gone?

September 12th, 2013

Joy where have you gone?

I have not left.

I am here within you.

You have forgotten you have wings.

You have covered them up with the cloak of your thinking.

Close your eyes and imagine them.

Do not be afraid, feel them.

They are Real.

Take off the cloak and feel the breeze upon your feathers.

They can take you anywhere.

Anywhere!

Fly, Fly . . . Fly

with the wings of your mind.

Feel the breeze of Joy on your face.

Whale by the Tail

September 13th, 2013

I've got a whale by the tail

Imagine it

Do it

Become it

Nothing is impossible

Surrender without Expectation

September 15th, 2013

Hands open and receptive

Reading Truth from the ancient book

Ready to receive

without need for her friend's understanding.

Seek first to understand

bonded one species to another

without need for words

Sharing

Loving

Beings

Intentions

November 10th, 2013

To listen with an ear to understand

To appreciate and inspire others

To cherish and support others

To move forward with a positive attitude

To provide encouragement for others growth

To accept change in others

To know that health and wellbeing is everyone's natural state

To see challenges as opportunities for everyone

To always treat others with respect

To know no one is greater or less than me

To joyously give and receive without expectation

To experience Joy without cause

Divine Stuff

October 20th, 2015

There is a Presence, a Power, a Force, an Energy, an Intelligence, a Divine Stuff from which everything is made. It is the mind of the sculptor, the hands of the sculptor and the completed piece of art. It can be called by many names. The name of this Divine Stuff is not nearly as important as is the recognition of it. Recognition is all important. In this sacred instant I recognize this Divine Stuff as the one source of all good in my Life. I recognize my unity with this Divine Stuff for I too am made of It. I am a microcosm of the macrocosm and thus I am a sculptor of my world with the Power to direct the hands of the Master Sculptor to create the art I desire in my Life.

I now fling open the door of my heart to new possibilities. I recognize opportunities. I work in harmony with the Master Sculptor's hands. I move forward with a positive attitude. I recognize health and well-being as my natural state. I give and receive in fulfillment of the law of circulation without the need for reciprocation because I trust the Law. I experience Joy without external cause. I rejoice in both my self reliance and my openness to honest communication. I am infinitely abundant in all areas of my life because the One Source of Divine Stuff in, through and as me is infinite!

Grateful for all the gifts that are right now present in my Life I give thanks for my openness to the ever upward spiral of good. Knowing my Life is Good and Very Good I release my word to the Sculptor's Hands. And so it is!

Values

October 27th, 2015

The Infinite Spirit is authentic, compassionate, playful and always acts with integrity. To speak of Spirit's connection is to not fully understand Spirits Oneness. For Spirit is the One Thing and how can the only One Thing be connected to anything else? It is already One, already Whole, already working in harmony as One Thing, fully complete within itself. In the words of Rumi "Even the phrase each other doesn't make any sense." In this moment I know this is the Oneness that I am. I am Whole. I am complete.

I am all the attributes of Spirit. Therefore I am an authentic playfully compassionate expression of Spirit who acts with integrity in my connection with others. I listen with an ear to understand. I appreciate and inspire. I cherish and support. I move forward with a positive attitude. I encourage others growth. I accept growth in others. I know that health and well-being is everyone's natural state. I see challenges as opportunities for everyone. I know that no one is greater or less than me and I am a team player. I give and receive because I trust the Law of circulation. I experience Joy without external cause.

Knowing this fills me with gratitude for all the authenticity, compassion, playfulness, integrity and connection in my Life while remembering that connection is a realization of the Oneness of my Life.

I release this into the Law knowing it is done. And So It is!

I Act Now

November 3rd. 2015

In the absolute of Spirit there is no such thing as past or future. There is only the eternal Now. All that is, exists in the ever-present Now. Every experience, every task, every expression, all that God is, expresses Now. God is all there is because Now is all there is. Now is simply another name for God. Therefore I too exist only in the Now. Everything I do, everything I have ever done, and everything I shall ever do, is done Now. Then was Now. Now is Now and any future is experienced Now.

Therefore the appearance of procrastination falls away because in a reality where there is no such thing as future, the concept of procrastination cannot exist. I can only do it Now. I consciously choose to act in harmony with Spirit in the relative world. I choose to do a task or not do it. There is no delay. I recognize the difference between the absolute Now and the relative world where man has created the concept of time and space. In the relative world I am a Wizard of time and space. I carefully choose my thoughts and recognize any avoidance or reluctance to perform a task as a message from that small still voice within to look deeper and question what I truly believe about the action I am avoiding and knowing that there is something deeper for me to understand. Knowing that through increased awareness I make better choices that manifest the Good that is already mine.

Grateful for the increased awareness and conscious focus on my wise choices I release my word into the Law knowing it done. And so it is.

I Ask

November 17th, 2015

I recognize the vast Cosmos as the infinite nature of God. God is limitless, all encompassing, stretching beyond all currently imagined limits. Numbers do not apply here. Infinite is beyond anything that can be counted. I open my mind to the Infinite. God is Wholeness, Kindness and boundless Supply. I release all boundaries in my recognition of the Universal One.

In recognizing God I am expressing as a unique individualized expression enmeshed right now in the Infinite Universe of which I am infinitely aware. In the words of Rumi I am not a drop in the ocean, I am the entire ocean in a drop. Knowing all that I recognize is also in, through and as me I know that all that I desire is already within me.

I affirm that through knowing my oneness with all that is, that the Universe always says yes and any limits are self-imposed so I now release all thoughts of lack. I affirm that asking is simply making my demand on a lawful Universe. I affirm that hearing someone say "No" is not rejection but only redirection to my Good. I affirm there is Good for me and I now recognize it in all its forms.

Grateful for my new openness to asking for what I want I know I am blessed. I am so grateful for both the **yes** and **no** responses for these are like signposts that guide me on the path to my Good. I am so very grateful to know my Good is vast and moving to me at Light speed.

Knowing this is simply a revealing of Truth I release my word into the Law. And so it is.

Clear Mind and Clear Life

December 8th, 2015

This is what I know. God, Spirit, Universe, Infinite Intelligence, Atman, Brahman, Mother Earth, Father God, The Cosmos, Heaven's Door, Creator, Infinity, The Divine, Jesus, Lord, Hosanna, Jehovah, Christ Consciousness, Buddha, Shiva, Power, Love, Wisdom, Truth, Beauty, Life, Supreme Being, Ultimate Clarity, Big Sweetie or simply It, no matter what I call It the principle does not change. It is all that is and the availability of everything known. Within the awareness of It, all is known. Nothing is beyond. All is included. All is possible.

Therefore I know I am included in this Infinitude.   I declare that nothing is beyond my grasp. I am clear in my dealing with every situation in my Life. I bring Light with me wherever I go. I am sitting on a goldmine and ready willing and able to share this fortune everywhere I go. Things that used to baffle me are now clear and I move with decisive action in grace and ease. All is well and I am ready for all that Life brings. It is GOOD and very good.

Grateful for this realization, grateful for the Peace, Joy and Clarity in my Life, I release my word into the Law. And so It is.